Growing Through Arts!

by Aleksandra ℠

THE
Snow Maiden
OPERA BY *Aleksandra* ®

MUSIC SERIES
BOOK 2

Illustrations by Elizaveta Efimova

Special Thanks to Russian Cathedral Ensemble, Mila Samokhina, Heather Aranyi, Golosa Choir, Nikolas Wenzel, Emily Becker, and Merit School of Music

Library of Congress Control Number: 2011934341
ISBN 978-0-9838325-1-5

Production Date: December 20, 2011
Printing Plant Location: Everbest Printing Co. Ltd.,
    Nansha, China
Job/Batch #: EPC-RN-103612.1

FROM *Aleksandra*®

The magic of an opera, the breathtaking sweep of a symphony, the rousing spirit of a musical . . .

Welcome to the Music Series from **Growing Through Arts**®!

One of the greatest treasures in human life is music. The impact of music on *children's* lives is especially powerful. Far beyond providing simple entertainment, music lays a foundation for success in academics, career, relationships, and life itself. Participation in the musical arts helps children develop critical skills such as spatial reasoning, fine motor movement, and language processing. At the same time, it builds vital character traits such as focus, discipline, confidence, creativity, respect for a teacher, and the ability to work independently and in a group.

It gives me special pleasure to share with you the timeless stories of Snow Maiden (Opera), Peter and the Wolf (Symphony), and Oliver Twist (Musical). In these delightful tales your child will be transported into the magical world of musical performance. Each story introduces new musical terms and performance concepts, but the learning doesn't stop there. Through uplifting storylines, the books also teach important life values, such as the need for courage and compassion; the rewards of hard work; the beauty of unconditional love; the value of overcoming fears; and the gifts of following your passions.

It is my deepest wish that these books provide countless hours of education, discovery, time-sharing, and meaningful conversation for you and your child. I hope in some tiny way they inspire your child to greater achievement and fulfillment, and empower him or her to be a better global citizen.

Thank you for making **Growing Through Arts**® a part of your lives!

Ever Growing Through Arts,
Aleksandra
www.aleksandra.com

How to Use This Book

🍂 Read the story to your child many times to encourage memory and to explore the themes more deeply.

🍂 Pretend you are in a theatre, listening and watching the "musical performance" unfold on stage!

🍂 Read and discuss Miss Aleksandra's Themes & Values, integrated throughout the book, and look for ways to relate them to your child's life.

🍂 Look for **bold words** in the story, and look up their meanings in Miss Aleksandra's Glossary. Help your child learn about music and the performing arts.

🍂 Create "teachable moments" with your child by learning letter- and music-themed words in the Music Alphabet by Aleksandra (sold separately), which integrates characters, concepts and story elements from the storybook.

🍂 Stage Scene Play Sets (sold separately) bring characters to life!

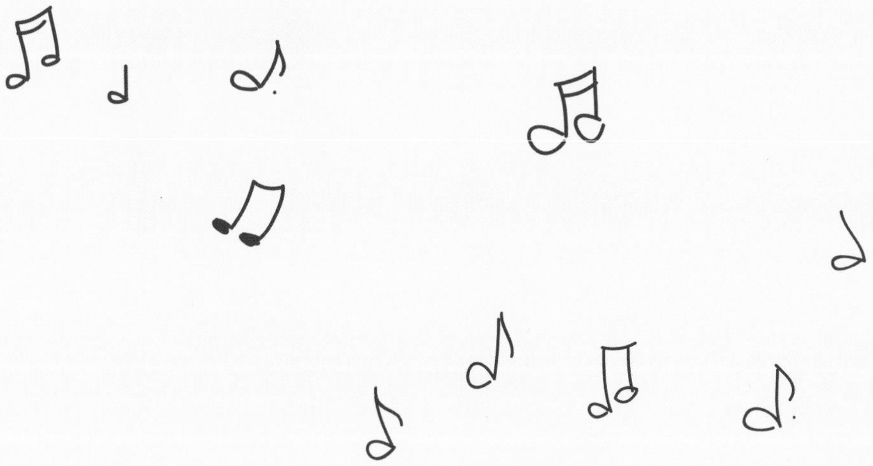

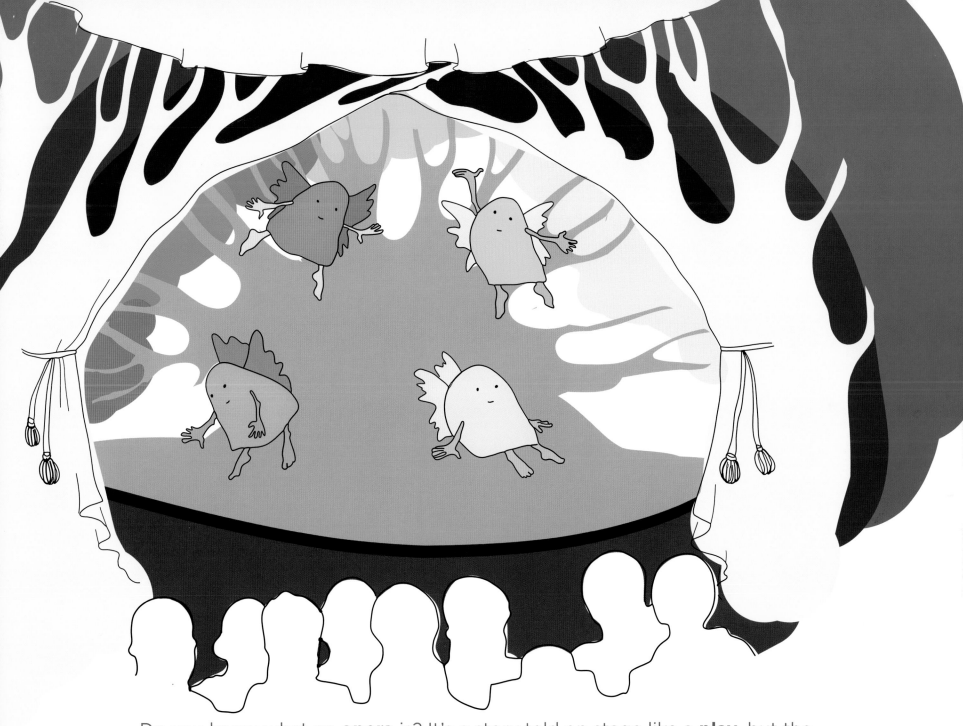

Do you know what an **opera** is? It's a story told on stage like a **play**, but the **characters** *sing* their **roles** instead of speak them!

Tonight we'll be seeing *The Snow Maiden*, an opera based on a Russian fairytale. This new **production** uses **classical** music, but the **lyrics** tell the story in a fresh new way.

The **overture** is playing! The opera is about to start! As the curtain rises, the first **scene** begins in a magical fairy kingdom . . .

Long ago, in a land in the clouds,
lived the Fairies of the Seasons.
Frost Fairy was the ruler of winter,
and he had a beautiful daughter
named Snowmaiden.

3

Snowmaiden loved her father and his frosty ice castle, but sometimes
when she closed her eyes, she could feel a warm
little light deep inside her.

Part of her loved that light, but part of her was afraid of it.
After all, she was a *winter* fairy. If she let her light grow
big and bright, it might melt her icy world.
So she just stayed in her cold,
cold castle, gazing out
the window.

☛ *Do you have your own special
"light" shining inside you? I'll bet
you do! Tell me about it!*

Bright Sun Fairy loved Snowmaiden and sang **arias** to her every day. Whenever she heard his warm **tenor** voice, the little flame inside her grew brighter and warmer.

Why does Snowmaiden's "light" grow brighter when she hears music? What makes the light inside you shine brighter?

6

This frightened Snowmaiden, and she would hide deep in the shadows.

Sun Fairy longed for her to come out and sing with him in the sunlight.

Frost Fairy could see that both of the young fairies were troubled and sad. At last he said to his daughter, "You must go and live in the world of humans, my dear. For that is where fairies learn to listen to their hearts."

Frost Fairy said goodbye to Snowmaiden, knowing he might never see her again.

A new stage set flies in from the **wings**.
Now we're in a snowy world of people!

In the human world, winters were long and cold,
and summers were short.

There was no springtime at all!

9

One day, Mr. and Mrs. Wood were out chopping logs in the icy snow.
They were dreaming about the daughter they'd always wanted.

"I think she would have been a singer," sang Mr. Wood,
"a great **prima donna**."

"I think she would have been a gardener,"
sang Mrs. Wood, "a grower of flowers."

 It's the most special gift for parents
to have a child. I'll bet someone
wanted to have you very much!

Mr. and Mrs. Wood tossed snow at each other playfully and began to sing a **duet** about their imaginary girl.
"Let's make her out of snow!" sang Mrs. Wood in a high **soprano**.
"Let's see if she will grow!" sang Mr. Wood in a rich **baritone**.

And that's just what they did. They made a girl out of snow!
When they were finished, they held hands and looked at her.

Do you think people ever get too old to play, laugh, pretend, and imagine? Do you know any older people who are still playful? Do you want to be playful when you get older?

Suddenly . . . a puff of breath came from the snow girl's mouth! 🍃

Her eyes blinked, and she said, "Hello, Mother and Father," with a voice as sweet as a robin's. Their snow girl had become real!

"We'll call you Snowmaiden," sang Mrs. Wood, happier than she'd ever been.

🍃 *Love can make "magical" things happen! Tell me about someone you love!*

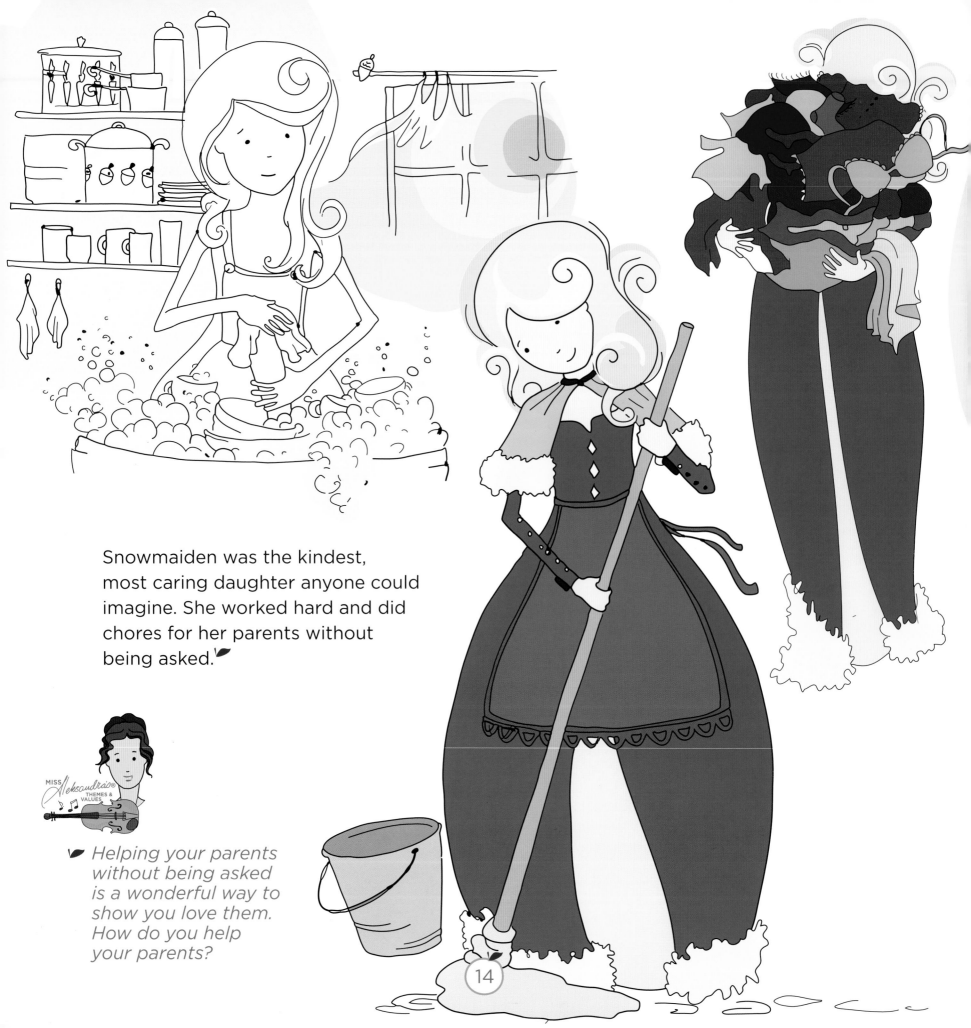

Snowmaiden was the kindest, most caring daughter anyone could imagine. She worked hard and did chores for her parents without being asked.

Helping your parents without being asked is a wonderful way to show you love them. How do you help your parents?

Her parents loved her very much, but sometimes
they would tell her, "You've done enough work
today. Go to the village. Sing! Dance!
Have some fun!"🍃

"I don't need to sing," Snowmaiden would reply.
"And I'm happy here in the house."
But every day, between chores, she gazed
longingly out the window.🍃🍃

🍃 *I think it's important to work hard
and* have fun, *don't you? What do
you work hard at? How do you
relax and have fun?*
🍃🍃 *Snowmaiden says* she's happy, *but
do you think she really is?*

One day, Snowmaiden heard
distant singing from the village.
Its soft **vibrato** caused a warm flutter in her chest.
"That's Lel," said Mrs. Wood. "He could melt an iceberg with
his voice. Go and listen to him. Don't be afraid. Go!"

The tenor notes sounded familiar to Snowmaiden and made
her feel strange inside. She felt as if a tiny fire was growing in
her heart. At first she wanted to run and hide, but the call
of the music was too strong to resist.

Snowmaiden grabbed her coat and scurried to the
village. She ducked behind a tree and watched Lel sing.
He reminded her of someone, in another time and
place, but she couldn't remember whom.

*When you really love something, like
music or dance or sports, it seems
to call to you, doesn't it? What kinds
of things call to you?*

MISS *Aleksandra's*® THEMES & VALUES

16

All she knew was that Lel's
singing made her feel
bright and warm.

She jumped out of hiding and began to dance.  Lel took her arm and spun her around. And then, for the first time ever, Snowmaiden began to sing. It was the most beautiful **tone** Lel had ever heard. Her voice blended with Lel's in perfect **harmony**. She felt the light inside her burning brighter and warmer, brighter and warmer . . .

"No!" she cried, stopping her song and dance. "I was made from snow. Such brightness is for others, not for me!"

When you feel excited about trying something new, it can make your fear disappear!

Sometimes you have to be brave enough to feel strange new feelings if you want to grow. Did you ever have a new feeling that scared or surprised you?

Snowmaiden ran home to her parents' house and hid in the cool shadows.

She went back to helping her parents, but she was afraid to leave the house again. She began to grow colder and paler by the day, as if she were turning back to snow again. Mr. and Mrs. Wood were very sad and worried.

Why do you think Snowmaiden felt afraid to leave the house again?

Meanwhile, Lel spent his days searching for Snowmaiden. He *had* to hear her voice one more time. He asked everyone in the village about her, but no one knew who she was or where she lived.

One day he was passing through the woods when he caught a glimpse of her pale face in a frosty window. He tip-toed up to the house and began to sing.

When Snowmaiden heard the song, the fire
in her heart began to glow again. "No,"
she whispered, "I'll burn too brightly!
Something bad might happen!"
But the more Lel sang, the less
she could resist. Finally she
stepped outside.

As she watched Lel singing warmly in the cool air, her feet began to dance. She couldn't stop them! Her mouth opened and she began to sing. All the villagers stopped what they were doing and rushed to hear the magical sound. Even the birds flew closer to listen.

As the **volume** of her singing rose, the light inside her grew bigger and brighter. This time she didn't try to stop it.

Soon, the villagers began to join her song. It swelled into a spectacular **chorus.**

Suddenly, the sun burst through the clouds, brighter than it had ever shone. The snow melted from the fields at once. The brightness from within Snowmaiden seemed to reach out and join as one with the rays of the sun. Warm color returned to her skin as the grass turned green and flowers bloomed.

When we let the light inside us shine, everyone around us wants to be part of it! How do you let the light inside you shine?

Snowmaiden felt her body changing, but it didn't frighten her.

She turned into a swirling mist and floated up to the sky.
"Goodbye, Snowmaiden," waved her parents,
wiping their eyes. "Goodbye, dear daughter, goodbye."

Lel waved, too, knowing that Snowmaiden
belonged in a different world.

The chorus reaches a **crescendo**, then fades to silence as the curtain closes and the **house lights** brighten. The **playbill** tells the story's final ending.

MISS *Aleksaudra's*®
THEMES & VALUES

☛ *Changing and growing are important if you want to do great things. That's why a caterpillar changes into a butterfly! What are some ways you want to change and grow?*

"Snowmaiden married her true love, the Sun Fairy, and became known by a new name: the Fairy of Spring. Now she and Sun Fairy sing together in the fields every day, teaching songs to the birds. And after every winter, she brings a warm, green spring to the world of humans.

"As for Snowmaiden's parents? They were sad to see her go, but happy for her, too. And every year she pays them a special visit. They see her face in the soft, white clouds of springtime and hear her voice in the song of birds."

MISS *Aleksandra's* THEMES & VALUES

By letting the light inside her shine, Snowmaiden became one of the greatest fairies of all. What great things will your *light* lead you to do?

Did you ever have two different feelings about the same thing? Sad and happy? Excited and worried? What made you feel that way?

MISS *Aleksandra's*® GLOSSARY

Glossary

COURTESY NIKOLAS WENZEL

baritone

RUSSIAN CATHEDRAL ENSEMBLE. PHOTO BY MILA SAMOKHINA

chorus

An **aria** is a beautiful song, full of feeling, usually sung by a single *character* (see below) in an opera.

Baritone is a man's singing range that is lower than *tenor* (see below) but higher than *bass*.

A **character** is a make-believe person played by a performer (see *role*, below).

When many singers sing together in an opera, they form a **chorus**.

Most **classical** music was composed over a hundred years ago. It uses traditional orchestra instruments such as violins, flutes, and French horns.

Music that slowly builds to a peak of loudness is known as a **crescendo**.

A **duet** is a song performed by two singers together.

When different notes or chords come together in a pleasing way, it's called **harmony**.

The **house lights** brighten the audience area of a theater. They are shut off during the performance.

The words sung in an opera or musical* are known as the **lyrics**.

Opera is a kind of stage performance in which a story is told through song. The performers *sing* all of their words instead of speak them.

An **overture** is a piece of music that plays before the action of an opera or musical* begins.

A **play** is a story performed on stage by actors.

The **playbill** is a printed program for the audience that has information about the performers, the story, and the show.

A **prima donna** is the main female singer in an opera company.

house lights

prima donna

The word **production** means a version of a play or opera performed by a particular company.

A **role** is a character played by a performer in a play, musical*, or opera. Sometimes a role is also called a *part*.

Operas and plays are made up of story "chunks" called **scenes**.

A female singer who sings in the highest range is using a **soprano** voice. The two lower female voice-ranges are called *mezzo-soprano* and *contralto*.

Male singers with a high voice-range sing **tenor**. The two lower male voice ranges are called *baritone (see above)* and *bass*.

Tone means the special quality of sound made by a voice or instrument.

When singers or musicians use **vibrato**, they "wobble" the pitch a little to create a rich, warm sound.

Volume means the loudness of music.

The **wings** of a theater are the spaces on the sides of the stage that the audience can't see.

*Learn about Musicals in the **Growing Through Arts**® book, *Twist, A Musical* by Aleksandra.

role

soprano

tenors

Make Every Moment a Teachable Moment!

GROWING THROUGH ARTS® COLLECTION

BALLET SERIES

The Nutcracker Ballet by Aleksandra®

The Cinderella Ballet by Aleksandra®

The Sleeping Beauty Ballet by Aleksandra®

The Nutcracker Ballet Practice & Play Book by Aleksandra®

The Cinderella Ballet Practice & Play Book by Aleksandra®

The Sleeping Beauty Ballet Practice & Play Book by Aleksandra®

MUSIC SERIES

The Snow Maiden Opera by Aleksandra®

The Peter and the Wolf Symphony by Aleksandra®

Twist, A Musical by Aleksandra®

INTERACTIVE LEARNING TOYS AND ACCESSORIES

For each beautifully illustrated storybook in the Ballet and Music Series, we offer several interactive learning companion pieces including Practice & Play Books, Stage Scene Play Sets, an Alphabet Set and dress-up accessories such as ballet slippers, tiaras, tutus, leotards and tights to bring the characters in the storybooks to life.

WWW.GROWINGTHROUGHARTS.COM

Aleksandra Efimova is the founder of **Growing Through Arts**® and President of Russian Pointe, a brand of luxury ballet shoes specially handcrafted and imported directly from Russia. Russian Pointe's flagship Russian Pointe Dance Boutique on Chicago's Magnificent Mile features the most sought-after pointe shoes and dancewear accessories as well as the entire Growing Through Arts Collection. Born in St. Petersburg, Russia, Aleksandra graduated from the renowned Art School at the Hermitage State Art Museum and received training in classical dance, art and academics. In 1993, she moved to the United States where she started her first successful company while still an undergraduate student. An Alumna of the prestigious Harvard Business School, she has dedicated herself to sharing access to and enjoyment of the arts, and to building bridges among people of different cultures. Her passion for the arts, Russian culture and international relations has helped propel Aleksandra Enterprises into the international spotlight as a company that transcends boundaries of language and culture. To learn more visit: **www.aleksandra.com**.

rough Art Grow

Grow

Growing Thro